D1305467

BUILDING ON A DREAM

THE
WHITE
HOUSE

Tamra B. Orr

PURPLE TOAD
PUBLISHING

Copyright © 2018 by Purple Toad Publishing, Inc. All rights reserved. No part of this book may be reproduced without written permission from the publisher. Printed and bound in the United States of America.

Printing   1   2   3   4   5   6   7   8   9

BUILDING ON A DREAM

Big Ben
The Burj Khalifa
The Eiffel Tower
The Empire State Building
The Golden Gate Bridge
The Great Wall of China

The Leaning Tower of Pisa
The Space Needle
The Statue of Liberty
The Sydney Opera House
The Taj Mahal
The White House

Publisher's Cataloging-in-Publication Data
Orr, Tamra B.
   The White House / written by Tamra B. Orr.
      p. cm.
Includes bibliographic references, glossary, and index.
ISBN 9781624693526
1. White House (Washington, D.C.)—Juvenile literature. 2. Architecture—Vocational guidance—Juvenile literature. I. Series: Building on a Dream: Kids as Architects and Engineers.
 NA2555 2017
 720

Library of Congress Control Number: 2017940647

eBook ISBN: 9781624693533

ABOUT THE AUTHOR: Tamra B. Orr is the author of hundreds of educational books for readers of all ages. A native of Indiana, she and her family now live in the Pacific Northwest. Orr graduated from Ball State University and has been writing nonstop ever since. In addition to learning about the world, she loves to go camping, and is known for reading five books at the same time.

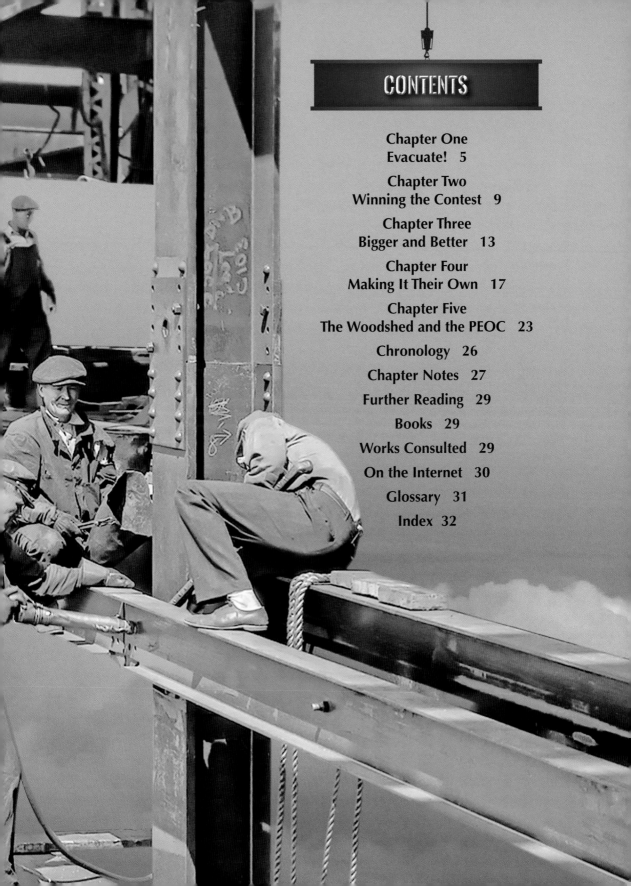

CONTENTS

Chapter One
Evacuate! 5

Chapter Two
Winning the Contest 9

Chapter Three
Bigger and Better 13

Chapter Four
Making It Their Own 17

Chapter Five
The Woodshed and the PEOC 23

Chronology 26

Chapter Notes 27

Further Reading 29

Books 29

Works Consulted 29

On the Internet 30

Glossary 31

Index 32

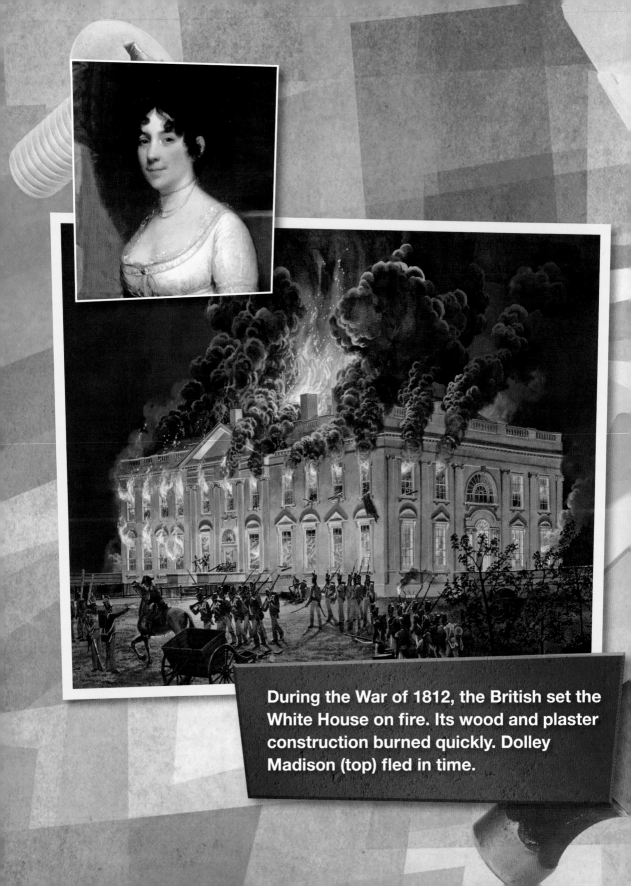

During the War of 1812, the British set the White House on fire. Its wood and plaster construction burned quickly. Dolley Madison (top) fled in time.

Evacuate!

The First Lady flew through the rooms of the White House, trying not to panic. Her husband, President James Madison, had warned her that the British troops were close. He hoped his wife had enough "courage or firmness" to wait for him to come back from battle.[1] If he did not return, she was to grab whatever she could and escape. Every few minutes, Dolley picked up the spyglass and scanned the horizon, searching for her husband. Instead, she saw British troops gathering. She knew what that meant. It was time to pack the most important items and get out. But where should she begin? Everywhere she turned there was a painting, a statue, or an antique that deserved to be saved. She looked longingly at the drawing room's red silk-velvet curtains. The White House was still so new, and it was already in great danger.

"Hurry, Dolley," she muttered. "He said to be brave and protect the most important things." Minutes later, the Declaration of Independence was in her hands. Now what? She looked at the full-length portrait of first president George Washington hanging on the wall. She knew the British would destroy it. Quickly, she had the portrait's frame taken down and broken. The canvas was carefully removed and rolled up. She sent it out of the White House for safekeeping. In a letter to her sister, Dolley wrote, " . . . and now, dear sister, I must leave this house, or the retreating army will make me a prisoner in it by filling up the road I am directed to take."[2]

The First Lady escaped and joined her husband in a nearby city. The Madisons were just in time. The very next day, August 24, 1814,

British soldiers stormed into Washington, burning the city as they marched.

the British arrived. Led by Rear Admiral Sir George Cockburn, 4,500 soldiers marched into Washington, D.C. It was 100 degrees in the city, with a threat of thunderstorms in the air.

Cockburn knew that the White House was open to attack. There were no guards posted outside. The only army in Washington was made up of volunteers, and they were gone. The admiral and his men invaded the building. They sat in congressmen's chairs and held a mock congress. "Who is in favor of burning?" Cockburn asked. "Aye!" replied all of his men.[3] Before starting the fire, the men took time to eat the feast that had been prepared for a fancy dinner party the Madisons had planned to host. Then the men stood up and dropped the first match. Moments later, fire tore through the White House.

For two years, the War of 1812 had raged on. The British had marched into Washington in order to embarrass President Madison and weaken the United States. As some of the most important buildings in Washington lit up the sky with the flicker of flames, the British watched with pride.

Their satisfaction was short-lived.

As Washington burned, the skies turned dark. Flashes of lightning lit up the sky, followed by rolls of thunder. The wind roared through the city, so powerful that riders were knocked off their horses. Rain drenched the city, putting out the flames. The British soldiers struggled to get back to their ships, rushing down muddy roads littered with broken tree limbs and other debris. Suddenly, a tornado ripped through the city. Roofs were blown from houses. Buildings were leveled. Two of the British ships were blown ashore.

According to history, at some point during the unexpected storm, a British officer turned to one of the city's residents and exclaimed, "Great God, Madam! Is this the kind of storm to which you are accustomed in this infernal country?" The lady replied, "No, sir, this is a special interposition of Providence to drive our enemies from our city." The officer shook his head and said, "Not so, Madam. It is rather to aid your enemies in the destruction of your city."[4]

By the next day, the storm was over and the city was left with blackened, burned buildings. Rumors spread throughout Washington that instead of rebuilding, the White House would be built in another city. Some predicted Philadelphia. Others thought it would be New York City.

In the end, both ideas were rejected. The Madisons returned to Washington and dedicated their lives to rebuilding their home. To bring it back to its original splendor, they turned to the one man who had designed and built it in the first place: Irish architect James Hoban.

White House Facts (2017)	
Number of doors	412
Number of rooms	132
Number of windows	147
Number of bathrooms	35
Number of fireplaces	28
Number of staircases	8
Number of elevators	3
Number of floors (basements, public floors, floors for the First Family)	6

The Samuel Osgood House in New York's Manhattan was the country's first Presidential Mansion. George Washington (top) and his family lived there for almost two years.

Winning the Contest

It is no surprise that so many people like to be part of contests. Who doesn't love the chance to compete, hoping to win the grand prize? That excitement is true today—and it was true more than two centuries ago. That's when Secretary of State Thomas Jefferson decided to hold a contest to see who would be given the chance to design the White House.

In 1790, Congress passed the Residence Act. It stated that this new country needed a national capitol building, along with a home for the acting president. The buildings were to be constructed within the next ten years. George Washington, the country's first president, would choose the site for this house. He thought about Philadelphia and New York City. In the end, his childhood memories helped him make the decision. The first president grew up along the Potomac River and loved it, so he chose Washington, D.C. Once the site had been selected, it was time to pick an architect.

On March 14, 1792, newspapers ran an ad written by Jefferson. It asked architects to send in their designs for a presidential home. President Washington stated that he wanted the American Presidential Palace, as it was being called, to have "the sumptuousness of a palace, the convenience of a house, and the agreeableness of a county seat."[1] Contestants had four months to submit their ideas. When that time was up, a handful of proposals had been received. The winning design came from James Hoban. He was an Irish architect who had come to

James Hoban

the United States as a teenager after the Revolutionary War. Hoban's vision for the president's home was based on the Leinster House back in Dublin, Ireland, where he had studied architecture.

The cornerstone of the future White House was placed on October 13, 1792. It took eight years for the home to be built. The construction team was made up of immigrants from several countries, including Scottish masons and Irish and Italian brick and plaster workers. Records also show that a number of African slaves were part of the team as well.

The building was made out of sandstone. This material was not only easy to shape and carve, but easy to access. The sandstone was brought to the site from a quarry on an island 40 miles away, rather than carried across great distances by huge cargo ships, trucks, or trains.[2] Crews chiseled the sandstone with small picks. Then, they used levers to move pieces onto oxen-pulled carts and sleds. From there the stone was shipped up the Potomac River to the construction site. More oxen-pulled carts toted the sandstone from the ships to where the builders needed it.[3]

In 1798, the building was coated with a lime-

President Washington watches as the cornerstone is laid in 1792.

The north side of the White House displays the symmetry in Hoban's design.

based whitewash—a color that would one day contribute to its permanent name. The paint was added to protect the sandstone from freezing during cold Washington winters. The paint was refreshed every few years. Finally, in 1818, the lime-based whitewash was replaced with white lead paint. Each time the building was painted, it required a staggering 570 gallons! It cost $235,372 to build the White House. That is equal to more than $4.4 million today.

Although sandstone was a good choice at the time, it proved to be a problem later on. After the British attack in 1814, the walls of the White House began cracking and pitting. It was time to call in James Hoban again. He returned to Washington and rebuilt the famous home nearly from scratch. A few of the original sandstone walls were kept, but everything else was replaced. It took three years to complete.

George Washington died before the first White House was completed, so he never got to live in it. Instead John and Abigail Adams were the first official residents of the Presidential Palace. They moved in on November 1, 1800. Paint was still drying, and rooms were still stark and quite damp and cold. The First Lady had to hang her wet laundry to dry in the empty East Room. That would not last long! It was time to make the White House grow and change along with the country.

Jefferson's floor plans, 1804. Renovations completed 100 years later included polished wood floors in the East Room.

PUBLIC DINING ROOM

dumbwaiter

PORTER'S LODGE

ENTRANCE HALL
(WILDERNESS MUSEUM)

UNFINISHED PUBLIC AUDIENCE CHAMBER

UNFINISHED STAIRCASE

CROSS HALL

LIBRARY (PRESIDENT'S OFFICE)

PRESIDENT'S ANTE-CHAMBER

OVAL DRAWING ROOM

PRIVATE DINING ROOM

MERIWETHER LEWIS QUARTERS (CANVAS WALLS)

STORE ROOM

BEDROOM

COMMON BED-ROOM

UNFINISHED STAIRCASE

CENTRAL HALL

VESTIBULE

DRESSING

PRESI-DENT'S BEDROOM

PRESI-DENT'S OFFICE

LADIES' DRAWING ROOM

SECRE-TARY'S OFFICE

OFFICE

Bigger and Better

From the very first time a president lived in the White House, the building has undergone changes. Some of the changes were necessary to keep the building strong and safe. New roofs and walls were added or repaired. Some of the changes were done in order to make the building bigger and more useful. Still other changes were made because of the personal preferences of each president. Incoming presidents changed paint colors. They chose a different decorating style or theme.

The Adamses had barely settled into the White House when they had to leave again to make room for the country's new president: Thomas Jefferson. The famous politician was startled to find the White House was still missing some walls and ceilings. He began making changes right away. He had water closets installed—an early form of bathrooms. This made it unnecessary to run outside to use the chilly outhouse. Jefferson also decided that the front entrance to the palace should be on the north side, so he had it moved. He added pavilions to the east and west sides of the home. They were used as homes for the servants and stables for the horses.[1]

A fan of the wilderness, Jefferson added mounted animal heads and Native American artifacts to the East Room and Entrance Hall. He had a stone wall built around the White House. He covered the grounds in trees, grass, and shrubs. Eager to show off the changes, Jefferson opened the doors for public tours in 1805.

During Madison's time in the White House, the British attacked, burning the building almost to the ground. Hoban returned and rebuilt the home. He came back again in 1825 and 1829 to add south and north porticos to the building. In the 1830s, running water and central heating were added. This made life in the White House much more comfortable. Gaslights replaced candles and oil lamps.[2] In 1891, electricity was finally added. President Benjamin Harrison and his family were so frightened of being electrocuted by touching the light switches, they made their servants turn the lights on and off every day. Many years later, President Lyndon B. Johnson (1963–1969) was just the opposite. He was known for turning off lights to save energy (even in rooms where people were working). It earned him the nickname "Light Bulb Johnson."[3]

As presidents came and went, they left their mark on the White House. Andrew Jackson (1829–1837) added a music room. When Millard Fillmore was president (1850–1853), he added a library. Other

presidents had brought books into the home, but they had taken them with them when they left. The Fillmores created a permanent library, selecting each book personally. Catherine Parisian, professor of English at Pembroke, stated at a conference at the Library of Congress, "Millard and Abigail

While Fillmore added the library, electric lights were not yet available.

The Game Room, 1992. Grant was not the only president who enjoyed billiards. Lincoln called the game "health inspiring."

Fillmore clearly valued books as an integral part of their lives."[4]

Ulysses S. Grant (1869–1877) had a billiards room built between the house and a brand-new iron greenhouse. In 1881, the White House got its first elevator. It was run by hydraulics. Seventeen years later, an electrical one replaced it.

President Harrison's wife, First Lady Caroline, had many ideas for expanding and improving the White House. She planned to add art galleries, guest rooms, presidential offices, and more greenhouses. Her plans came to an end when the bill for the expansion did not pass Congress.

The concept of remodeling and extending the White House was only briefly considered by Harrison's successor, Grover Cleveland (1885–1889; 1893–1897). He was followed by William McKinley (1897–1901), who was not excited about the idea at all. His wife was known for saying, "There won't be any hammering while I live here."[5]

As the century came to an end, the White House was showing signs of wear and tear. Visitors touring the home were known for cutting pieces of fabric to take home with them. During open houses, people had stood on furniture, tearing and staining the pieces. The home was 100 years old. It was time to spruce it up and make some changes. President Theodore Roosevelt (1901–1909) was just the man to do it.

The Oval Office was originally George Washington's idea. He wanted it to be the main room in which presidents greeted visitors. Theodore Roosevelt (left) added a new wing for his family.

Making It Their Own

Theodore Roosevelt gets credit for securing the White House's name. For years, the building had been called a presidential palace or executive mansion. Thanks to Teddy, the name White House stuck. Roosevelt became president very quickly when William McKinley was assassinated. When he moved into the White House in 1901, he brought along his wife, Edith, and their six children. With his children underfoot, being president was difficult, so Roosevelt built the West Wing. This helped him separate his work and living quarters, so he could work in peace. With his family on the second floor, he quickly installed extra bathrooms.

Roosevelt also built a one-story office structure connecting to the White House. When William Taft (1909–1913) followed Roosevelt, he enlarged the office, creating the White House's Oval Office. (Although the White House has had an oval office since Washington's planning stage, this new one in the West Wing became the official Oval Office we think of now.) Roosevelt also added an East Wing to the grounds. It was specifically for use when many guests visited. There was plenty of room nearby for cars and carriages. Even better, the wing had a huge cloak room big enough for all of the guests' coats and hats.

During World War I, Woodrow Wilson (1913–1921) wanted to support the war. He filled the South Lawn with grass-munching sheep. This saved the cost of paying staff to mow it. The sheep's wool was auctioned, earning thousands of dollars for the Red Cross. While the sheep were a good idea, they ate too much grass. According to *The*

The sheep were bothered by the constant traffic coming to and from the White House.

Atlantic, the sheep had "eaten up nearly all the grass in the rear." When the animals were moved to the front yard, the grounds' flower beds were in trouble. By August, the *Washington Post* stated, "President Wilson [had] decided to retire from the sheep business."[1]

One day, in 1927, President Calvin Coolidge (1923–1929) was in the White House's attic when it began raining heavily. He was shocked to see how leaky the roof was! Quickly, he ordered it repaired, adding steel girders and turning the attic into a full third floor.

Two years later, on Christmas Eve, a fireplace flue stuck in one of the White House's 28 fireplaces. President Herbert Hoover was hosting a children's Christmas party at the time. Fire rushed through parts of the White House, gutting parts of the West Wing and the Oval Office. Several of Hoover's aides ran to the president's office, removing desk drawers and steel cabinets. Secret Service agents grabbed Hoover's chair and the presidential flag. Dozens of fire trucks rushed to the White House, and more than 100 firefighters worked to put out the blaze. Fire hydrants as far as five blocks away helped supply the water needed to extinguish the flames. Freezing temperatures made everything more difficult. Finally, the fire was out. It took four months for the repairs to be finished. President Hoover and his wife moved back in on April 14.[2]

When Franklin D. Roosevelt, or FDR, (1933–1945) came to the White House, one thing became clear. The building had not been made for a president in a wheelchair. Ramps were added, elevators were updated, and a heated indoor pool for his medical therapy was built. The pool was enjoyed by later presidents, including Harry S. Truman (1945–1953) and John F. Kennedy (1961–1963). When Richard Nixon (1969–1974) became president, he had the pool taken out. Then Gerald Ford (1974–1977) had a pool built outdoors. Today, that pool is still used. It now has a pool house for changing clothes. A special underground tunnel allows the First Family to go to the pool without going outside. Under FDR, the White House's large coatroom was turned into a movie theater.

Harry Truman's daughter Margaret played the piano. One day, a leg on her piano broke through the floor. It was the final sign to Truman that the White House needed major repairs, as he had suspected. Chandeliers shook. Floors swayed. Walls cracked. According to Margaret's autobiography, construction experts came in to survey the damage and stated nothing could be saved but the outside walls! "The entire house would have to be gutted

The White House pool (shown here in 1963) used to be indoors.

Chapter 4

President Nixon and his wife were big fans of bowling. They had a one-lane alley built for their use in 1969.

and rebuilt," she wrote.[3] The Truman family moved across the street to Blair House while the White House was rebuilt from the inside out. Wood was replaced by concrete and steel beams. New walls and ceilings were installed. The repairs took from 1948 to 1952 and cost $5.7 million.

As the years passed, the changes in the White House continued, including some specifically for fun. Nixon had a bowling alley built in the basement. Eleanor Roosevelt had playscapes built for her 13 grandchildren. The Kennedys installed swing sets and jungle gyms for their children, John and Caroline. Jimmy Carter built a treehouse for his daughter, Amy. The Obamas put in swing sets on the South Lawn for daughters Malia and Sasha. Barack Obama also added movable basketball hoops on the tennis courts.

Putting hoops in the tennis courts made it possible to use the same space for two different sports.

Michelle Obama hoped the White House Kitchen Garden project would live on as a symbol of "the hopes and dreams we all hold of growing a healthier nation for our children."[4]

What do cabbages and figs have to do with the White House? Thanks to Jefferson and then generations of First Ladies, the White House also has gardens. For years, fruit and vegetables were grown on presidential grounds, but the tradition faded after World War II. That tradition was brought back when Michelle Obama began her Let's Move fitness program for young people. To encourage kids to eat healthy, Obama planted a 2,800-square-foot garden. Up to 2,000 pounds (one ton) of produce comes from this garden each year, feeding the staff and White House guests. "The garden is really an important introduction to what I hope will be a new way that our country thinks about food," the former First Lady said. "That's the story of the garden. And it's been quite an amazing success, if I do say so myself."[5]

Two of the most secret, high-tech, and intense places in the White House are the PEOC (top) and the Situation Room.

The Woodshed and the PEOC

Perhaps two of the most exciting and mysterious places in the White House are the Situation Room, sometimes referred to as "The Woodshed," and the PEOC, or President's Emergency Operation Center. Both of these spots have been shown in movies and television shows many times. They usually show up along with tense situations, worried actors, and action-filled plots. These two locations are often confused. However, they have different purposes. They are also located in different places. The Situation Room is in the basement of the West Wing. The PEOC is under the East Wing.

The first emergency bunker was built for FDR in 1942. He wanted it to be an air-raid shelter plus a secure meeting place in case of emergency. The bunker was expanded during Truman's renovations. A tunnel was built connecting the East and West wings. Almost twenty years after the bunker was built, John F. Kennedy was struggling with an international conflict known as the Cuban missile crisis. He worried that the information he was getting was not always trustworthy, so he created the Situation Room. In 1987, Ronald Reagan had another tunnel built for protection in case of terrorist attacks. It allowed a president to reach a secret staircase simply by pressing on a wall panel that, in turn, opens a secret door.[1]

The Woodshed is 5,000 square feet. It was updated in 2006. It was outfitted with flat-screen television sets and technology capable of linking the president and his staff with other officials around the world. It has five secure video rooms. The room also has a direct feed to the president's plane, Air Force One. Privacy booths for phone calls and windows with privacy glass make it possible to share information without fear of being overheard by anyone.

Michael Bohn, former manager of the Situation Room during the Reagan administration, told Politics Confidential, "Once you go in there, you can't take your cell phone in. . . . If you want to talk on the phone, you have to go into an old-fashioned phone booth that closes, sort of like the Clark Kent cabinet."[2]

The soundproof room is kept under 24/7 surveillance by a team from the National Security Council.[3] One door in the Situation Room leads directly to the pool and pool house. The "Sit Room" is where politicians gather to watch, learn, and discuss a current crisis. The personnel see live feed from government drones and other cameras. This is where Barack Obama and his staff were during the hunt and capture of terrorist leader Osama bin Laden.

The PEOC is where the president and other important staff are taken in the case of an emergency such as a terrorist attack or invasion. The PEOC is built strong enough to withstand a nuclear blast. This is where Vice

The president and his advisers were able to watch the capture of Osama bin Laden (in Pakistan) from the Situation Room.

The White House with the Washington Monument and Potomac River behind it

President Dick Cheney and other important staff were taken following the attacks of September 11, 2001. Like the Situation Room, the PEOC has the most high-tech equipment. It allows staff to monitor events and communicate with others, including foreign countries, the Central Intelligence Agency (CIA), the Department of Defense, and Homeland Security. It is manned 24/7 by military officers. Getting in requires going through multiple vault doors.

The White House has been part of this country's history for hundreds of years. It is not perfect, however. It constantly requires repairs. It needs ongoing care and maintenance, as well as technology upgrades. As each presidential family comes and goes, the look of the White House changes. Rooms are redone. Colors shift. Decorating styles come and go. But one thing stays the same. The White House remains a symbol of the United States and its people.

1791 George Washington chooses the site for the American Presidential Palace, what will come to be called the President's House, and then the White House.

1792 James Hoban wins the design competition, and the cornerstone is laid.

1800 John and Abigail Adams move into the unfinished White House.

1805 Thomas Jefferson opens the White House for public tours.

1814 During the War of 1812, British troops burn the White House and other government buildings to the ground.

1830 The portico is completed for the north or main entrance of the building.

1879 The East Wing is completed.

1881 The first White House elevator is installed.

1891 Electricity is installed.

1901 White House restoration project begins. The West Wing is built.

1909 The West Wing is doubled in size.

1913 First Lady Ellen Axson Wilson creates the White House Rose Garden.

1929 Fire guts part of the West Wing.

1933 The first White House swimming pool is installed.

1942 Franklin Roosevelt creates an underground bomb shelter. He builds a home movie theater and offices above it.

1947 A bowling alley is built on the ground floor of the West Wing.

1949 A huge renovation on the White House's structure begins.

1952 The Trumans move back into the White House after the residence is rebuilt.

1961 Jacqueline Kennedy adds a portable stage in the East Room for White House performers. She updates and redecorates the private living quarters. After the Cuban Missile Crisis, President Kennedy builds the Situation Room.

1962 *Tour of the Executive Mansion* is aired on CBS. It has a record audience of 56 million viewers.

1977 First Lady Rosalynn Carter places her personal office in the East Wing. Since then, the East Wing has served as office space for the first lady and staff.

1979 President Jimmy Carter installs the first solar panels on the White House.

1987 Ronald Reagan has another tunnel constructed under the White House. It is meant to protect the President and his staff in case of terrorist attacks.

1992 Computers with Internet access are installed in the White House.

2002 George W. Bush has 167 solar panels installed to generate electricity for the White House.

2006 The Situation Room is updated and expanded.

2009 Barack Obama remodels the tennis court into a basketball court. Michelle Obama sponsors the Let's Move project, which includes expanding the White House gardens.

2017 First Lady Melania Trump hires designers for the White House. Gold curtains, reflecting the décor of Trump Tower, are hung in the Oval Office.

Chapter 1

1. History.com Staff. "Dolley Madison Saves Portrait from British." History.com, 2009. http://www.history.com/this-day-in-history/dolley-madison-saves-portrait-from-british

2. Ibid.

3. The White House Historical Association. "Saving History: Dolley Madison, the White House & The War of 1812." Undated. https://www.whitehousehistory.org/teacher-resources/saving-history-dolley-madison-the-white-house-and-the-war-of-1812

4. Federer, Bill. "The Storm That Saved the Nation's Capital." *Smithsonian Magazine.* March 15, 2017. http://www.smithsonianmag.com/science-nature/the-tornado-that-saved-washington-33901211/#CxulKBUjbzDxwx7o.99

Chapter 2

1. NNDB. "James Hoban." Undated http://www.nndb.com/people/633/000204021/

2. U.S. Geological Survey, "Famous Building Stones of Our Nation's Capital." Undated. https://pubs.usgs.gov/fs/2012/3044/pdf/fs2012-3044_rev432012.pdf

3. Krishnamurthy, Kiran. "Sandstone in Washington Buildings Came from Island on Aquia Creek." *Baltimore Sun.* September 30, 2002. http://articles.baltimoresun.com/2002-09-30/news/0209300244_1_aquia-creek-government-island-small-island

Chapter 3

1. "Jeffersonian Enhancements: 1801–1809." The White House Museum. http://www.whitehousemuseum.org/special/renovation-1801.htm

2. "Architectural Improvements: 1825–1860." The White House Museum. http://www.whitehousemuseum.org/special/renovation-1825.htm

3. Lantero, Allison. "The History of Electricity at the White House." Energy.gov. October 14, 2015. https://energy.gov/articles/history-electricity-white-house

4. Cole, John. "Fillmore's Foundation." Library of Congress. July/August 2010. https://www.loc.gov/loc/lcib/10078/library.html

5. Profiles of U.S. Presidents. "The White House—Restoration." Undated. Profiles of U.S. Presidents. http://www.presidentprofiles.com/General-Information/The-White-House-Restoration.html

Chapter 4

1. Resnick, Brian. "White House Sheep, a History." *The Atlantic.* October 17, 2014. https://www.theatlantic.com/politics/archive/2014/10/white-house-sheep-a-history/453405/

2. Treese, Joel D., and Evan Phifer. "The Christmas Eve West Wing Fire of 1929." The White House Historical Association. https://www.whitehousehistory.org/the-christmas-eve-west-wing-fire-of-1929

3. Truman, Margaret Daniel. "The White House Was Falling Apart." Harry S. Truman Library and Museum. https://www.trumanlibrary.org/whistlestop/qq/ds2_4b.htm

4. Rosner, Elizabeth, and Marisa Schultz. "Michelle Obama Pushes for an Executive Order to Preserve White House Garden." *New York Post*, November 8, 2016. http://nypost.com/2016/11/08/michelle-obama-pushes-for-an-executive-order-to-preserve-white-house-garden/

5. Taylor, Lisa Hallett. "21 Fun Facts about the White House's Outdoor Spaces." *The Spruce.* January 22, 2017. https://www.thespruce.com/facts-about-white-houses-outdoor-spaces-2736705

Chapter 5

1. White House Info. "The Underground White House." https://whitehouse.gov1.info/tunnel/

2. Hurt, Charles. "New White House War Room Loaded with Gadgets." *New York Post.* May 19, 2007. http://www.pressreader.com/usa/new-york-post/20070519/281552286429018

3. "Situation Room." White House Museum, n.d. http://www.whitehousemuseum.org/west-wing/situation-room.htm

Further Reading

Books

Arnold, Tedd. *Fly Guy Presents: The White House.* New York: Scholastic Reader, 2016.

Herrington, Lisa. *The White House.* New York: Children's Press, 2014.

House, Katherine. *The White House for Kids: A History of a Home, Office, and National Symbol, with 21 Activities.* Chicago, Il: Chicago Review Press, 2014.

Rhatigan, Joe. *White House Kids: The Perks, Pleasures, Problems, and Pratfalls of the Presidents' Children.* Watertown, MA: Charlesbridge, 2015.

Sabuda, Robert. *The White House: A Pop-Up of Our Nation's Home.* New York: Orchard Books, 2015.

Smithsonian Institution. *The Smithsonian Book of Presidential Trivia.* Washington, D.C.: Smithsonian Books, 2013.

Stine, Megan. *Where Is the White House?* New York: Grosset & Dunlap, 2015.

Works Consulted

Cole, John. "Fillmore's Foundation." Library of Congress. July/August 2010. https://www.loc.gov/loc/lcib/10078/library.html

Federer, Bill. "The Storm that Saved the Nation's Capital." *Smithsonian Magazine.* March 15, 2017. http://www.smithsonianmag.com/science-nature/the-tornado-that-saved-washington-33901211/#CxulKBUjbzDxwx7o.99

History.com Staff. "Dolley Madison Saves Portrait from British." History.com. 2009. http://www.history.com/this-day-in-history/dolley-madison-saves-portrait-from-british

Hurt, Charles. "New White House War Room Loaded with Gadgets." *New York Post.* May 19, 2007. http://www.pressreader.com/usa/new-york-post/20070519/281552286429018

Krishnamurthy, Kiran. "Sandstone in Washington Buildings Came from Island on Aquia Creek." *Baltimore Sun.* September 30, 2002. http://articles.baltimoresun.com/2002-09-30/news/0209300244_1_aquia-creek-government-island-small-island

Lantero, Allison. "The History of Electricity at the White House." Energy.gov. October 14, 2015. https://energy.gov/articles/history-electricity-white-house

NNDB. "James Hoban." Undated http://www.nndb.com/people/633/000204021/

Profiles of U.S. Presidents. "The White House—Restoration." Undated. *Profiles of U.S. Presidents.* http://www.presidentprofiles.com/General-Information/The-White-House-Restoration.html

Resnick, Brian. "White House Sheep, a History." *The Atlantic*. October 17, 2014. https://www.theatlantic.com/politics/archive/2014/10/white-house-sheep-a-history/453405/

Taylor, Lisa Hallett. "21 Fun Facts about the White House's Outdoor Spaces." *The Spruce*. January 22, 2017. https://www.thespruce.com/facts-about-white-houses-outdoor-spaces-2736705

Treese, Joel, and Even Phifer. "The Christmas Eve West Wing Fire of 1929." The White House Historical Association. https://www.whitehousehistory.org/the-christmas-eve-west-wing-fire-of-1929

Truman, Margaret Daniel. "The White House was Falling Apart." Harry S. Truman Library and Museum. https://www.trumanlibrary.org/whistlestop/qq/ds2_4b.htm

U.S. Geological Survey, "Famous Building Stones of Our Nation's Capital." Undated. https://pubs.usgs.gov/fs/2012/3044/pdf/fs2012-3044_rev432012.pdf

White House Historical Association, The. "Saving History: Dolley Madison, the White House & The War of 1812." Undated. https://www.whitehousehistory.org/teacher-resources/saving-history-dolley-madison-the-white-house-and-the-war-of-1812

White House Info. "The Underground White House." https://whitehouse.gov1.info/tunnel/

White House Museum. "Architectural Improvements: 1825-1860." The White House Museum. http://www.whitehousemuseum.org/special/renovation-1825.htm

White House Museum. "Jeffersonian Enhancements: 1801-1809." The White House Museum. http://www.whitehousemuseum.org/special/renovation-1801.htm

White House Museum. "Situation Room." http://www.whitehousemuseum.org/west-wing/situation-room.htm

On the Internet

Fact Monster
https://www.factmonster.com/us/national-landmarks/white-house

"Weird Things You Didn't Know about the White House"
https://www.kidsdiscover.com/quick-reads/weird-things-didnt-know-white-house/

White House Facts
https://www.scholastic.com/teachers/articles/teaching-content/white-house-facts/

"White House Facts/15 Interesting Facts about the White House"
http://mocomi.com/white-house/

White House Facts for Kids
Kidshttp://factsforkids.net/white-house-facts-for-kids/

architecture (AR-kih-tek-shur)—The design of buildings.

artifact (AR-tih-fakt)—A tool or object made by a human.

assassinate (uh-SAS-ih-nayt)—To murder, usually for political reasons.

auction (AWK-shun)—To sell to the highest bidder.

billiards (BIL-yurds)—A table game of hitting balls into pockets using a cue stick.

debris (deh-BREE)—Trash or broken pieces.

electrocute (ee-LEK-troh-kyoot)—To kill or injure by a burst of electricity.

fire hydrant (HY-drunt)—A firefighter's emergency water connection.

flue (FLOO)—A tube or pipe used as an outlet to carry smoke away from a fire or boiler.

girder (GIR-dur)—A large supporting beam.

hydraulic (hy-DRAW-lik)—Driven by fluid.

interposition (in-ter-poh-ZIH-shun)—A barrier; something that comes between.

mason (MAY-son)—A person who works with stone.

pavilion (puh-VIL-yun)—Part of a building that juts out from the rest; a separate, decorative building.

portico (POR-tih-koh)—A covered entrance to a large building.

quarry (KWAH-ree)—An open area for mining stone.

renovate (REH-noh-vayt)—To make something like new again; update.

sumptuousness (SUMP-choo-us-ness)—Showing extreme cost, richness, or splendor.

symmetry (SIH-mih-tree)—Balance among parts; the quality of having two sides that reflect each other's shape, size, and design.

PHOTO CREDITS: Back cover—WEBN; p. 8—NIH.gov; pp. 12, 18—loc.gov; p. 16—ObamaWhitehouse.Archives; p. 19—Robert Knudsen; p. 21—NPS.gov; p. 25—Glyn Lowe. All other photos—Public Domain. Every measure has been taken to find all copyright holders of material used in this book. In the event any mistakes or omissions have happened within, attempts to correct them will be made in future editions of the book.

Adams, Abigail   11, 13

Adams, John   11, 13

bin Laden, Osama   24

Bohn, Michael   24

British attack   4, 6–7, 11, 14

Carter, Jimmy   20

Central Intelligence Agency   25

Cheney, Dick   25

Cleveland, Grover   15

Cockburn, Sir George   6

Coolidge, Calvin   18

Department of Defense   25

Fillmore, Abigail   14–15

Fillmore, Millard   14

Ford, Gerald   19

Grant, Ulysses S.   15

Harrison, Benjamin   14

Harrison, Caroline   15

Hoban, James   7, 9–10, 11, 14

Homeland Security   25

Hoover, Herbert   18–19

Jackson, Andrew   14

Jefferson, Thomas   9, 13

Johnson, Lyndon B.   14

Kennedy, John F.   19, 20, 23

Leinster House   10

Madison, Dolley   4, 5

Madison, James   5–7, 14

McKinley, Edith   17

McKinley, William   15, 17

National Security Council   24

Nixon, Richard   19, 20

Obama, Barack   20, 24

Obama, Michelle   21

Potomac River   9, 10

Reagan, Ronald   23

Red Cross   17

Residence Act   9

Roosevelt, Eleanor   20

Roosevelt, Frank D.   19, 23

Roosevelt, Theodore   15, 16, 17

Samuel Osgood House   8

Taft, William   17

Truman, Harry   19

Truman, Margaret   19–20

War of 1812   6

Washington, George   5, 8, 9, 11

White House

   construction   10

   contest   9

   cornerstone   10

   cost   11

   East Wing   17

   elevators   15

   expansions   13, 14

   fire   18

   gardens   21

   library   14–15

   PEOC   22, 23–25

   pool   19

   public tours   13

   sheep   17–18

   Situation Room   22, 23–24

   West Wing   17

Wilson, Woodrow   17–18